D0168753

# A Cloud
# Of Witnesses

Sermons On 10
Who Jesus Touched

## Gordon Pratt Baker

CSS Publishing Company, Inc.
Lima, Ohio

# A CLOUD OF WITNESSES

Copyright © 1994 by
The CSS Publishing Company, Inc.
Lima, Ohio

**Library of Congress Cataloging-in-Publication Data**

Baker, Gordon Pratt.
    A cloud of witnesses : cameos of ten who testified / by Gordon Pratt Baker.
        p.     cm.
    ISBN 1-55673-516-2
    1. Bible. N.T. — Biography — Sermons. 2. Jesus Christ — Biography — Public life — Sermons. 3. Sermons, American. I. Title.
BS2431.B35     1994
225.9'22—dc20
                                                                            93-30841
                                                                            CIP

ISBN 1-55673-516-2
PRINTED IN U.S.A.

*This is for my wife,*
*Dorothy Elizabeth Baker,*
*who for nearly half a century*
*so graciously bore with me*
*the burning of the noontide heat*
*and*
*the burden of the day.*

*... we are surrounded by
so great a cloud of witnesses.*
— Hebrews 12:1

# Contents

Introduction 7

An Outcast:
*Woman Of Samaria* 9

A Scholar:
*Nicodemus* 15

A Lady With A Listening Ear:
*Mary Of Bethany* 21

A Wilderness Prophet:
*John The Baptist* 27

A Mother:
*A Canaanite Woman* 33

A Big Fisherman:
*Peter* 39

A Woman Of Substance:
*Mary Magdalene* 45

A Patriot:
*Dysmas* 51

A Family Member:
*Salome* 57

A Quiet Man:
*Andrew* 63

A Cloud Of Witnesses 69

# Introduction

He lived in a small, occupied, Eastern country which he left only once when taken in infancy to refuge in a strange land. (Matthew 2:1, 13-15) Until he was 30 he was shrouded in obscurity with but a single boyhood incident breaking through. (Luke 2:41-42; 3:23)

His mother was a pious peasant woman widowed in his youth and, as the oldest male in the family, he found himself charged with responsibilities beyond his years. For perhaps a little more than a decade he worked as a carpenter, fashioning plowshares and yokes, (Matthew 11:29-30) but by no means limited to such labors, undoubtedly devoting numerous hours to repairing out building houses in his own and neighboring towns. Evenings he spent tallying accounts or studying the Torah. Sabbaths he "went to the synagogue as his custom was." (Luke 4:16)

How vividly he recalled the plain little house in which he grew up with colorful vines clinging to the walls and with its flat mud roof. Many, indeed, had been the times after a hard rain when he had pressed the rutted surface back into shape with the cylindrical stone every householder kept on hand for the purpose. Many, too, were the occasions it had provided him a vantage point for watching the tumbling flight of rollerbirds and the antics of swallows darting among nearby olive trees.

Come spring he never tired of scaling the heights rising above his hometown to feast his heart on the splendor of pink phlox and wild geraniums carpeting the land falling away at his feet. Here, too, he thrilled to the sight of his country's three sacred mountains, Tabor, Hermon, and Carmel — timeless testimonials to God's way with his people — where "the alchemy of sunsets transformed gray and barren hills into monuments of gold."

All in all, he reflected, it had been a simple, satisfying life, marked with its problems, to be sure, and knowing its portion

7

of tears. But also there had been its moments of ringing laughter and always its rich friendships.

His name was Jesus, and his cause was humanity.

It was a cause Jesus did not have to meet alone. There was a cloud of witnesses to bear him out.

## An Outcast
# Woman Of Samaria

Intent on avoiding even the appearance of competing with John, whose disciples the Pharisees had goaded into a quarrel with his own, Jesus decided to withdraw from Judea to pursue his mission in Galilee. To do so, however, he must either travel by way of Perea, fording the Jordan twice as many of his countrymen did, or cross the full length of Samaria, which divided the two provinces. It was a choice of no mean significance inasmuch as the Jews and the Samaritans had long since severed relations with bad blood between them.

Because the Samaritans had intermarried with their Assyrian conquerors, the Jews had denounced them as a mixed breed, impure before the law, and therefore to be held in contempt. Moreover, they crowned this conviction by denying the Samaritans a part in the rebuilding of the temple, angering them to such a degree that they built their own temple on Mount Gerizim. As a result a bitter feud had developed between the two peoples, putting at risk any Jew making his way into Samaria.

It was a risk with which Jesus was all too familiar. Nevertheless he determined to take it in the interest of his mission. Consequently, he set out for Galilee early in the morning when the hours were cool for traveling, arriving probably about noon at Jacob's Well near the village of Sychar.

## I

Jesus had sat beside the well only a short time when he saw a woman, a water jar on her shoulder, plodding through the noontide heat toward him. Even before she reached him he knew she was an outcast. Her very presence at this hour told him so.

Traditionally the time for drawing water was the cool of the evening shortly before sunset when soft breezes were blowing. Besides, the years had made it a social hour providing the village women a welcome break in the day's occupation. (cf. Proverbs 31:15, 18) Yet here the woman came with never a glance behind her, walking a stranger in her own land.

Placing her jar on the stone coping of the well, the woman uncoiled the goat's-hair rope looped about her forearm, tying one end to the handle of her crock. Then, hand over hand, she lowered the vessel until she felt its added weight in the water. When she pulled the crock up it brimmed over, spilling a small puddle at her feet.

Only then did Jesus speak. He had had a long morning under a hot sun, and he was parched. So he asked the woman for a drink.

It was a daring thing to do, not simply because she was a Samaritan and an outcast, but because she was a woman; and his request astounded her. Surely, she must have thought, this strange Jew was familiar with the laws of his own people! Had not the rabbis decreed that "A man should hold no conversation with a woman in the street, not even with his own wife, lest men should gossip?" Besides, his obvious need notwithstanding, how dare he breach the wall of separation dividing their two peoples? Castaway she might be, but she was still a Samaritan and she would be met as one. Thus, taking no pains to conceal her scorn, she faced Jesus and asked him sarcastically, "How is it that you, a Jew, ask a drink of me, a woman of Samaria?" (John 4:9)

## II

Early in life Jesus had learned that the best way to meet a contentious spirit is to ignore it. Accordingly, he refused to be drawn into the sleeveless argument the woman was attempting to provoke. Instead he surprised her by replying, "If you knew the gift of God, and who it is that is saying to you, 'Give me a drink,' you would have asked him and he would have given you living water." (John 4:10)

10

Jesus was speaking figuratively. But the woman was a literalist. So she failed to catch his meaning despite the fact his metaphor should have been clear to her. From time immemorial the presence of water in a barren land had betokened the outpouring of God's sustaining grace. (cf. Psalm 23) But so deep-seated was the woman's prejudice against Jews that all she could hear was an audacious rabbi disparaging the patriarch who had bequeathed the well to her people.

Accordingly, her eyes flashing angrily, the woman sarcastically rebuked Jesus. "Sir," she said, pointing with a sneer to the stone-enclosed shaft, "you have nothing to draw with, and the well is deep; where do you get that living water? Are you greater than our father Jacob, who gave us the well, and drank from it himself, and his sons, and his cattle?" (John 4:11)

The woman had chosen her bait adroitly, for most Jews would have risen to it heatedly, their attention diverted from the woman to the ancient rivalry between their two countries. But Jesus was not about to be so easily diverted. There was, he knew, but one way to reach the woman. He must make her see he was interested in her, not as a Samaritan, but as a person. So, letting her jibe pass, he directed the discussion to her need.

"Every one who drinks of this water," Jesus said, glancing toward the well, "will thirst again; the water that I shall give him will become in him a spring of water welling up to eternal life." (John 4:13-14) He was, of course, speaking symbolically as a means of offering the woman his continuing concern and support. Even as he spoke, however, the woman's eyes gleamed with a cunning that robbed her of his meaning. Curling her lips in ridicule of his metaphor she scoffed, "Sir, give me this water that I may not thirst, nor come here to draw." (John 4:15)

### III

To the Occidental mind what Jesus did next seems irrelevant. He bid the woman call her husband. The directive surprised her. Nevertheless, her conscience twinging, she resolved in self-defense to brazen things through. "I have no husband," she replied.

The response was true as far as it went. But it also gave Jesus the opening he sought. For years of dissipation had etched their testimony on the woman's face.

"You are right in saying, 'I have no husband,' " Jesus rejoined, "for you have had five husbands, and he whom you now have is not your husband." (John 4:16-18)

It was a thrust the woman had not anticipated, and her insolence wilted with it. Surely, she thought, only a prophet could have known what Jesus did about her. Yet how different this prophet was! For unlike Samaria's prophets here was One whose very manner bespoke concern for even the likes of her! It was enough to set the woman thinking about her better self.

# IV

Still the woman could not resist one final ploy. "Our fathers worshiped on this mountain," she said, lifting her hand toward the 3,000-foot height of Gerizim, "and you say that in Jerusalem is the place where men ought to worship." (John 4:20)

Some have felt the woman was attempting a diversion at this point by using her national religion as a shield against Jesus. It seems more likely, however, that she was raising a question which, by both its tone and its nature, indicated the first sign of a readiness to be taught.

Child of her people, the woman had been told from her earliest days that Gerizim was the original site of Paradise. It was here, according to her Samaritan traditions, that God had fashioned Adam in his image, that Noah had beached the Ark, and that Abraham had prepared Isaac for sacrifice. Nor had her elders ever tired of forecasting the day when Gerizim would become the Messiah's steppingstone to establish his earthly kingdom.

It was an inheritance hard to ignore, as Jesus well understood. So, too, he understood the woman's obvious effort to
confirm it with him. But the very effort indicated her insights
could be broadening. So he seized it to bring her his final revelation.

"Woman," Jesus said, his voice reflecting the patience of
a parent speaking to a child's curiosity, "believe me, the hour
is coming when neither on this mountain nor in Jerusalem will
you worship the Father .... But the hour is coming and now
is, when the true worshipers will worship the Father in spirit
and truth, for such the Father seeks to worship him. God is
spirit, and those who worship him must worship him in spirit
and truth." (John 4:21-24)

Here at last was something the woman could grasp. How
often in the rainy season she had seen a mountain stream over-
flow its bounds and run unchecked across the desert to rouse
the barren land into bloom. (cf. Isaiah 35:11) Could the divine grace be any more constricted to Jerusalem or Gerizim
than the stream to the mountain? (cf. 1 Kings 8:27)

Salvation, the woman suddenly realized, is not of the shrine
but of the heart; and that being so "whosoever will" wherever one is may receive it. It was an exhilarating thought, and
with it a new and daring idea trembled on the verge of the woman's mind — an idea so big it must be too good to be true.
Could the weary rabbi smiling at her beside Jacob's Well be
the long-awaited Messiah? Reason sought to shout the notion
down. But the woman's heart refused to relinquish it. Thus,
almost before she knew it, she found herself saying, "I know
the Messiah is coming (he who is called Christ); when he comes,
he will show us all things." (John 4:25) The words were barely past her lips when she heard the reply, "I who speak to you
am he." (John 4:26)

Instantly the outcast forgot she was an outcast and, aban-
doning her water jar, she ran as fast as she could the half-mile
to Sychar to witness to her neighbors that the Redeemer had
come. And so tellingly did she bear her testimony that, losing
sight of the fact they had been ostracizing her, they followed

her to the well to hear Jesus for themselves. As a result, because of the woman's witness Jesus spent two days evangelizing in Sychar to let loose his gospel in Samaria. (John 4:39-41)

# A Scholar
## Nicodemus

When Nicodemus enters the gospel story he is already elderly (John 3:4) and well-to-do. (John 19:39) That he was an aristocrat his membership in the Sanhedrin attests. For not only was it the governing body of the Jewish people, its constituents were drawn from the priestly families of the land, the scribes, and the teachers of the law.

A recognized scholar, (John 3:10) Nicodemus was the kind of person who would die learning. Accordingly, unlike many of his colleagues, he kept an open mind to life, convinced that God had not spoken his last word or commissioned his last messenger. Indeed, such was his passion for truth that he pursued it wherever it might take him or through whomever it might come. Accordingly, he did not hesitate to mingle with the crowds clamoring to hear Jesus and what he heard convinced him that he should talk with the Master privately. For whatever else he may have been Nicodemus was a troubled man.

### I

On being enlisted in the Sanhedrin Nicodemus had been quickly elevated to its leadership. The high council had three officers, a president, a vice president, and a master, who was also known as "the wise man." It was this third-ranking-office to which Nicodemus had been elected, and to assure its proper administration he had steeped himself in the ethical moralism of the prophets.

At the same time, however, Nicodemus' position in the council entangled him in the practices of its conniving president, the crafty Caiaphas. To be sure, Nicodemus had protested the practices, for Caiaphas took pains to promote his crass schemes when Nicodemus was absent on council business elsewhere. Nevertheless, the very fact Nicodemus was an official of the body perpetrating Caiaphas' evil deeds had led him to fear he bore the taint of its president's guilt by association.

It was a sobering fear and, left to his own thoughts, Nicodemus could not shake it. Indeed, he apparently spent hours vainly agonizing over it. As a consequence he had come to the conviction he could not discharge the fear alone. So, impressed with what he had seen of Jesus, he decided to seek the Galilean's counsel. Nor would he have found it difficult to do so. For the Master was pursuing a practice common in Israel that would have provided Nicodemus easy access to him.

## II

Itinerant Eastern teachers regularly selected well-trafficked spots as stands from which to propagate their doctrines. It was a custom Jesus had adopted early in his ministry. Thus, he appealed to his hearers where he found them — by the seashore, (Matthew 13:1-2) on a mountainside, (Matthew 5:1) in a field, (Luke 6:17) on a street corner (Matthew 13:26) — even in the crowded courts of the temple. (Matthew 26:55)

Consequently, as Nicodemus went about Jerusalem on business for the Sanhedrin he must have encountered Jesus many times. A word in passing was all he would have needed to set up an appointment for the two to talk. The conjecture finds substance in the fact Nicodemus found in the dark the house where Jesus was staying.

Moreover it was probably Nicodemus who proposed midnight as the time for meeting. Certainly, there would have been good reason for the suggestion. For one thing, he would escape the heat of the torrid Palestinian day — in itself no mean consideration. Again, as one in the public eye, he was sensitive to the influence his action might have on any who chanced to see him enter the house for his rendezvous with Jesus. Accordingly, until he knew more about the Master's situation he would proceed cautiously. In addition he probably feared that a daylight call might unwittingly play into the hands of

Caiaphas' secret police by subjecting Jesus to arrest where there would be no one to defend him.

Inasmuch as Jesus had no place of his own the house where Nicodemus met with him was very likely John's. Scripture tells us the beloved disciple owned a home in Jerusalem (John 19:27) and undoubtedly, like Martha's and Mary's house at Bethany, it must have been available to Jesus whenever he desired its use. In addition, the exchange John reports between the two men suggests the Evangelist, while taking no part in the evening's encounter, nevertheless silently witnessed it.

## III

The interview itself, as John recounts it, is highly revealing, not only because it serves as a vehicle for one of the profoundest teachings in scripture, but equally because of what it tells us about Nicodemus.

For one thing, the interview clearly indicates that Jesus trusted Nicodemus. The Master was only too well aware of the Sanhedrin's passion to do away with him. Yet here he was sharing a quiet rendezvous with its third-ranking member. He who "knew what was in man" (John 2:25) was confident that Nicodemus would not betray him. So the midnight meeting attested the scholar's character as much as his passion for truth.

For another thing, we see here not the high-powered official whom many must have both hated and envied for the post he held, nor the pundit whose reputation preceded him wherever he went, but the man — the sincere, down-to-earth, cautious individual who readily recognized his shortcomings and earnestly desired to do something about them. Indeed, Nicodemus' very manner before Jesus manifests a humility which the role traditionally attributed to his rank has tended to conceal.

Reluctant to believe the Almighty had spoken his last word or unfolded his last secret, Nicodemus was willing to sit at the feet of a carpenter "not yet 50" (John 8:57) whom Jerusalem's leaders were labeling an ignorant man. (John 7:15) Nor was it a small concession on his part to do so. For one thing by seeking Jesus' counsel he was acknowledging that a Galilean untrained in the schools was as much a teacher from God as the proud priests of Israel. For another he was consulting that Galilean on basic points of Jewish theology, thereby reversing their allotted roles in life, in itself an intolerable act. Yet on neither count did Nicodemus hesitate to risk appearing naive by asking that carpenter the questions that were troubling him. (John 3:1-10) It was an act which, in the light of Nicodemus' official role, took no small courage.

Nicodemus was a Pharisee; (John 3:1) and, like all Pharisees, he had been steeped in an exclusive and Puritanical outlook on life. But not once in the course of their session together did Jesus call on him to renounce the harsh attitude and equally harsh actions of the body to which he belonged.

The omission is highly suggestive in view of the Lord's scathing denunciations of the sect as a whole for its vicious and often fraudulent ways. (Matthew 23:13-36; Luke 11:12-44) Instead, Jesus asked of his midnight visitor only that he commit himself to stir up the gift of God that was within him. (John 3:3)

It was a request Nicodemus was bent on honoring when he went out into the dawn.

## IV

Nicodemus had barely left Jesus' presence when he found himself challenged to make good on his resolution. To the consternation of the Pharisees Jesus' popularity had continued to grow. In fact, there was common talk that he was the King the Jews had been so long anticipating. (Mark 15:12) The very idea was freighted with emotion and might all too easily launch a messianic movement spawning an insurrection. Let Caesar get wind of it and his legions would pounce on Israel like eagles swooping up prey from a plain. (John 11:48)

18

Here was a situation that must be curbed at all costs, and Caiaphas lost no time in hatching a plot to do it. Not only would his stratagem convince Rome of the council's loyalty, it would also strengthen the council's control over the Jews. All that was needed, he told the Sanhedrin, was to seize and execute Jesus as an enemy of the state. Once the empire saw how quickly the Jewish leaders dealt with any who threatened the interests of their overlords the nation — and, with it, the council — would be free of the specter of disaster. (John 11:49-50)

Aware he was outvoted even before he spoke, Nicodemus nevertheless opposed the plot. "Does our law judge a man without first giving him a hearing and learning what he does?" he protested. (John 7:50-51)

It was a bold challenge, and even as he raised it Nicodemus knew it would bring the Sanhedrin's wrath upon his head. So he was not surprised when the high priest's veiled threat came. "Are you from Galilee, too?" Caiaphas snarled. "Search and you will see that no prophet is to rise from Galilee." (John 7:52)

There was no mistaking Caiaphas' meaning. Galilee had long since been a hotbed of rebellion. Had not Herod been repeatedly forced to quell the wild mountaineers there as they tried to drive their rulers into the sea? Let Nicodemus beware lest he, too, suffer Rome's vengeance.

At the same time, however, neither was there any mistaking the high priest's distrust of the protesting scholar standing Jesus' sole defender before him. Nor was he long in acting on that distrust.

Taking advantage of one of Nicodemus' absences — in all likelihood again on a trip for the council — and secure in the contempt the Pharisees held for the common people, Caiaphas sent soldiers under cover of darkness to seize Jesus and rush him to trial before dawn. The high priest and his cohorts were not about to have Nicodemus sitting as their conscience when they put Jesus to death.

What followed constitutes one of the most courageous testimonials in history.

## V

It was shortly after three o'clock on Friday afternoon, the seventh of April, 30 A.D. Joseph of Arimathea had courageously besought Jesus' broken body from Pilate to ensure its proper burial — an act in itself constituting open witness of commitment to Jesus — while Nicodemus had brought myrrh and aloe to the extent of 100 pounds to enhance the last fond rites for the dead (John 19:38-42) in a manner befitting One whose life had so profoundly touched their own.

It was a bold witness, openly defying a pompous ruler who could be a deadly foe and putting at stake all the two were or ever hoped to be.

Nor did Pilate permit the witness to pass unscathed. For tradition tells us that for his part in Jesus' burial Nicodemus was stripped of his post in the Sanhedrin and banned from Jerusalem. Yet despite such consequences, like another loyal follower long centuries later, Nicodemus had succeeded in declaring to Caiaphas and the world that:

> *I saw him once — he stood a moment there.*
> *He spake one word that laid my spirit bare.*
> *He grasped my hand, then passed beyond my ken.*
> *But what I was, I shall not be again.*

## A Lady With A Listening Ear
# Mary Of Bethany

There are as many ways to witness as there are witnesses. Not everyone can be like Andrew, who never met a stranger, or Peter, whose eloquence brought thousands to Jesus. (Acts 2:14-42) But one thing is sure. Each of us has a witness to bear.

### I

For Mary of Bethany the witness took the form of the hours she spent at Jesus' feet. It was an act of devotion the very sight of which must have spoken as tellingly to her neighbors as anything she might have said to them. It was not that she would have been content merely to sit mutely before Jesus. On the contrary. She would undoubtedly have lost no opportunity to share with her neighbors the gist of her conversations with him.

Granted, there were always the Twelve to whom she might expect the Master to turn when he felt the need to talk. But they were so involved in what was happening that they frequently lost sight of the forest for the trees. (Mark 9:30-32; Luke 18:31-34; John 10:6) Mary, on the other hand, had no such difficulty. For she had long since developed a sensitivity to the needs of others, like Walt Whitman attesting centuries later:

> *I do not ask the wounded person how he feels,*
> *I myself become the wounded person.*

So Mary could listen to Jesus receptively, hearing behind his words the dreams and the disappointments, the concerns and the commitments that pursued his days. As a consequence she could respect his silences, supporting them with her own and thus reverently affording him the reassurance he needed that he was understood.

Inevitably the hours Mary had thus devoted to Jesus had sharpened her own perceptive spirit. For as he spoke her vision of the kind of world he had come to establish both broadened and deepened, welling up in her a determination to do all she could in support of his appointed mission. Nor did she permit the determination to lie fallow. If she could be a listener, then why not a witness? After all, who could introduce others to Jesus more effectively than one who lived his dreams with him? But even more than that, Mary had a ready-made field of operation in which to do so.

With her sister Martha and her brother Lazarus Mary lived in a village approximately two miles from Jerusalem at the base of the Mount of Olives, which was popularly held to be the "foot-stool of God." Consequently there was a steady flow of pilgrims to it along the three roads converging at her door just a Sabbath day's journey from Jerusalem. Nor was there any let-up in the traffic the roads carried since tradition held that David had worshipped God on the Mount at a site offering no mean attraction to the pious. To Mary such an unbroken procession offered an opportunity for witnessing too good to ignore. So together with her brother Lazarus and her sister Martha she had pursued an open-door policy welcoming into their Bethany home any who had become fatigued or footsore.

It was an ideal setting for witnessing; for having already demonstrated an interest in the individual to whom she was providing the opportunity to rest she could feel free to go a step farther and share with her guest a stirring testimonial to Jesus. To be sure, she would have done it quietly and gracefully as befit her nature; but she would have done it no less tellingly, encouraging the individual to speak a good word for Jesus wherever he or she went.

It is speculation, of course, but who is to say that at least some of the saints welcoming Jesus into Jerusalem on the day of his triumphal entry may not at some point have experienced the hospitality Mary and her kin had tendered weary travelers at their Bethany hearth?

# III

Only once, so far as the scriptures tell us, did Mary witness to Jesus publicly. Beginning what was to prove his last journey to Jerusalem the Master had apparently made arrangements to spend the Sabbath with Mary's little family and their friends, confident that in their home he would not only obtain the rest he so sorely needed, he would also share heartwarming exchanges such as only good friends can stimulate to lift the spirit. In addition — for a while, at least — it would shield him from the ominous circumstances he had been warned were building up against him.

It was six days before the Passover and to show their affection for Jesus his Bethany friends decided to spread a banquet in his honor. Actually, it was to be the Sabbath festive meal and accordingly open to the public. So it promised to be a memorable event.

Simon the Leper — so-called because sometime in the past he had fallen victim to Palestine's most dreaded disease — was asked to host the meal. (John 12:1) That he would carry its scars to his grave goes without saying. But he must have been ritually free of it at the time of Jesus' testimonial dinner. Otherwise no Jew would have dared to eat with him, not only for fear of contracting the awesome ailment, but equally as much for fear of becoming ceremonially unclean by reason of association and thus barred from society. (Leviticus 13:45-46)

Mary's sister, Martha, was asked to cater the meal and promptly agreed to do so, calling upon a corps of her friends to assist her with it. Undoubtedly she had enlisted their help in similar situations before, so their group expertise offered Simon assurance of a memorable evening.

At the same time, however, Martha's acceptance of the responsibility without involving Mary in it barred Mary from the festivities since protocol dictated that only men might share the meal as guests.

For all the occasion's colorful trappings and joyous atmosphere, however, Jesus realized only too keenly that he was experiencing one of his last peaceful moments. For weeks he had been on the move, hounded from one place to another by enemies who even now lurked in the shadows of Simon's gates. (John 12:10) The pleasant feast spread before him and buzzing with lively fellowship, interrupted at times by bursts of boisterous laughter, was only an interlude in the chase as when a winded stag, momentarily eluding its pursuers, pauses to refresh itself at a mountain stream, all the while alert to the grim death poised just beyond its haven.

It was not that Jesus was ungrateful for the display of devotion the banquet was presenting on the part of his friends. It was rather that he was experiencing the sense of loneliness a crowd may unwittingly intensify.


## IV


Meanwhile, alone in Martha's house, Mary discovered she could not permit such a high moment in Jesus' life as the banquet being given in his honor to pass without manifesting her devotion to him. So she hastened to her room and took from her hoarded perfumes an alabaster vial of Indian spikenard — so named after the spiked flower from which it was extracted. Imported at no small cost she had been holding it for just such an occasion as this.

Accordingly, casting her customary decorum to the winds Mary raced the short distance to Simon's crowded house; and, bursting into Jesus' presence, she broke the colorful seal on the gleaming vial and anointed his head and feet with its fragrant contents. Then, falling to her knees before him, she loosed her long tresses — pride of any Jewish maiden and symbol of her purity as she came to her bridal chamber — and dried his feet with her hair. (John 12:3)

It was a bold move, suddenly and surprisingly made, that could easily have been taken for the voluptuous advance of a courtesan. But this woman whom everybody in Bethany knew — indeed, whom they admired and respected from her youth —

intent only on honoring Jesus and at the same time on bringing him solace in a trying hour never hesitated for a moment in doing what she did. Rather, so worshipfully did she fulfill her purpose that not even Martha, for all her practical bent, stood unmoved before Mary's display of devotion.

Nor did any other soul present but one.

Judas objected. "Why was this ointment not sold for 300 denarii," he asked, "and given to the poor?" (John 12:5) Unlike all the others witnessing the incident the man from Kerioth was blind to Mary's symbolism. Anointings were performed at coronations; (1 Samuel 10:1) and so far as Mary was concerned Jesus was the King of kings. Moreover, to her he would always be that. Not even death could end his sovereignty for her. For life, she was convinced, does not end at the grave since love does not end there. Hence Mary was proclaiming to all standing about her — and beyond them to the world — that Jesus would be the King of her life through all the days it pleased God to give her.

It was a proclamation that must have come to Jesus as one bright spot in a darkening hour. For it assured him that whenever his time came, and in whatever manner, he would be loved to the end. Nor would his cause die with him, the proclamation assured. (Matthew 26:13) For his mission of love would live on in the love of persons like Mary.

*A Wilderness Prophet*

# John The Baptist

---

John the Baptist was born to bear witness that Jesus was the Christ. (John 1:6-8) Like Jeremiah before him, while he was yet in the womb the Almighty anointed him to prepare the way of salvation for Israel. (Jeremiah 1:4-5; Luke 1:13-17) And what a dramatic witness he made. For he came to his calling as if he were the last of the Old Testament prophets. (Luke 16:16) Certainly, he must have looked the part the day he burst from the bare Judean hills — his long hair streaming, his black eyes blazing — to proclaim to the world that the long-awaited Messiah had come. (Matthew 3:1-3)

**I**

Here was no "reed shaken by the wind." (Matthew 11:7) Here was a herald who had come unscathed through the austerity of the desert with lightning bolts scoring crags above his head, sandstorms lashing hapless travelers, brigands pouncing on unwary victims, and death in the guise of vipers lurking behind every rock. Moreover, when the moment for action had struck, whatever its nature, he seized it with the tenacity of a hawk snatching its prey, pinioning its challenge with a moral judgment as piercing as that bird's talons.

Undoubtedly such a passion for the spiritual on John's part stemmed from his earliest days. For both his father, Zechariah, and his mother, Elizabeth, were priests of the order of Aaron, a lineage of no lesser distinction.

At the same time, however, for reasons of his own, John had not followed in their footsteps. Instead, he had taken to the desert to prepare himself for a lifetime of witnessing and while there he had met other men who, like himself, were searching its solitude for the key to more significant lives.

Strong personality that John was it did not take him long to band them together in the cause of righteousness and, returning with them, to travel the countryside evangelizing. And so effectively did he and his men do so that "Jerusalem and all Judea" were baptized by him in the Jordan. (Matthew 3:5) But in the process John performed the sacred rite for none until he was assured their commitments were genuine. (cf. Matthew 3:7-10)

## II

Cousins, (Luke 1:36) Jesus and John had grown up together. Accordingly, they had long shared a close relationship. In all likelihood, as with most childhood companions, they must have constantly run in and out of one another's houses munching tasty morsels fresh from their mothers' mud ovens or hunkered down side by side over some fishing hole, jointly displaying their catches with pride. How often, too, their chores done, the two of them must have joined the village children at play until some sulking youngster put an end to their games. (Luke 7:32)

Youthful experiences have a way of sealing the bonds binding one heart to another. So it was no coincidence Jesus was there when John came down to the Jordan preaching his gospel of repentance.

What surprised John was not Jesus' presence at the start of his ministry, but that the Master asked to be baptized. At first, knowing Jesus as intimately as he did, John protested. "I need to be baptized by you, and do you come to me?" he asked, (Matthew 3:13) thereby bearing open witness to the multitude that a greater person than he stood in their midst. The very thought of baptizing Jesus was awesome to him. Yet neither could John bring himself to deny the Master's request. Mulling it over later, however, he came to see it was Jesus' way of identifying with him (cf. Hebrews 4:15) and to have had even a small part in such a magnificent gesture was glory enough for anyone.

Meanwhile Israel's Tetrarch, a man named Herod Anti-pas, was becoming increasingly agitated over what he saw developing. For not only had Jesus' presence among the people been a disturbing factor to him, now John the Baptist was stirring them up too with his fiery preaching. Thus, to Herod the makings of a revolution were present and he must take decisive steps to quell it in the bud. Not knowing where else to start he sent a deputation of priests and Levites to check John out. Was John himself the Christ, Herod wanted to know. (John 1:24)

## III

The deputation's very question provided John with a perfect opportunity to witness for Jesus, and he was quick to pounce upon it. Speaking in a voice all could hear he replied, "Among you stands one whom you do not know, even he who comes after me, the thong of whose sandal I am not worthy to untie." (John 1:19-27)

At this late date John's words sound innocuous enough. But actually they constituted a bold witness to the Lord in the presence of potentially ruthless enemies. For they cut across the highest levels of Israel's status-conscious society, as a third century rabbi's instruction clearly indicates when he tells his coterie of young men, "Every service which a slave performs for his master a pupil will do for his teacher, except unloosing his shoe."

To Herod's emissaries John's reply was a full and unqualified commitment to Jesus, exalting him even above a ruler bent on preserving his prestige and power regardless of whomever he must destroy to do so or whatever price he must pay for it.

Nor did John's witness end there. At times, as he readily understood, one is called upon to witness to his own, not always the easiest witness to bear, but none the less vital than any other. Thus, John was not surprised when his followers began to ply him with questions about Jesus.

To the chagrin of those who had joined ranks with John, Jesus was drawing larger crowds than he, exciting their jealousy. It could have been a vexing moment for any man. But not for John. Instead, he seized the situation to undergird the commitments of his followers by apprising them of his place in God's plan, assuring them that all was going according to a heavenly design.

After all, was not John the forerunner sent to prepare the way while Jesus was the Messiah whose advent John was appointed of heaven to announce? Thus, was it not his divine mandate to make ready the way for the Lord's preeminence? And that being so, must it not follow that "He must increase, but I must decrease." (John 3:25-30) In short, did not the very increase in Jesus' ranks prove John was doing what God had sent him into the world to do?

It was the testimony of a prophet made with the forthrightness of a prophet. Moreover, it was a testimony drawn from years of sharing experiences with Jesus as the two of them had grown up together. For had not Jesus opened his innermost thoughts to John in days long flown as they had sat beside a favorite fishing hole or thrilled to the dancing of lilies of the field in the wind?

Nor could John have associated so long with Jesus, "who knew what was in man," (John 2:25) without coming to possess some measure of such knowledge himself. Thus, it is little wonder others listened when John spoke about Jesus. As Charles Francis Potter reminds us, "All the gospel writers agree that what started each out on his public ministry was the preaching of John the Baptist."

John did not limit his witness to words, however. Instead, he confirmed it by directing to the Master the latter's first two disciples. (John 1:35-37)

## IV

It was only a short time, however, until the skein ran out for John. Undoubtedly, there were two reasons for it.

30

First of all, as John's followers multiplied, Herod Antipas became increasingly uneasy. For he saw in John's growing numbers the threat of an insurrection.

The concern was not totally groundless, not because John was politically minded but because the times in general were uncertain marked as they were with numerous uprisings stemming from various messianic claims. Consequently, so far as Herod saw John's activities, far from being spiritually motivated, they were openly seditious, and with the crowds attracting larger and larger numbers to John, the Tetrarch felt he must take drastic action before John snatched Galilee from his control. Indeed the very thought of that happening made him shudder. John, he told himself, must be silenced before the unthinkable could come to pass by way of a rebellion John might spark.

In the second place, by scouring the region with his call for repentance, John was fast becoming Herod's conscience with nowhere to hide from it by day or by night. It was enough to drive one mad and somehow, the Tetrarch told himself, he must find a way to rid himself of it.

Meanwhile, however, Herod involved himself in a scandal with his brother's wife. It was customary for local administrators at Antipas' level to pay ceremonial visits periodically to the emperor. The occasion might be any significant occurrence at court. On one of these official trips — perhaps a death in Tiberius' family — Herod accepted his brother Philip's gracious invitation as house guest, then promptly rewarded the fraternal hospitality by stealing Philip's wife, Herodias.

True to form, John denounced Herod for his immorality. Nor did he do so from afar. Rather, he charged the lecherous ruler with his sin to his face. (Mark 6:17-18) It was more than Antipas could bear. So, goaded on by his partner in the sordid affair — and tricked into making her an infamous promise — he had John beheaded. (Mark 6:19-29)

It was an act to haunt Herod day and night. For try as he may he could not blot the horror of his deed from his mind. So persistently did it pursue him, in fact, that when Jesus swept

31

into Galilee to take up the work John's witness had prepared for him Herod was terrified at the thought John had returned from the dead to wreak vengeance upon him. (Luke 9:7)

# *A Mother*
# **A Canaanite Woman**

Like the woman of Samaria the mother from Canaan whose story Matthew and Mark have preserved for us was a foreigner. Tradition calls her Justa and names her daughter Bernice. One scholar describes her as "by language a Greek, by nationality a Canaanite, and by residence a Syro-Phoenician." So, too, she was probably Greek by religion. Coming from the Phoenician coast as she did she was very likely a member of a seafaring family.

## I

More to the point, however, the woman belonged to a race the Jews held accursed. And well they might have been. To be sure, the prophet Zechariah had foretold the day the Canaanites would become "like a clan in Judah." (Zechariah 9:7) But up until Jesus' time there had been no such lifting of the barriers between the two peoples.

Nor was there likely to be. For Canaan was a hotbed of religious cults given to fertility rites and snake worship. So, too, practicing black magic, it equipped its altars with sensual figures and made religious prostitutes an established order. All of which the Jews regarded as blasphemy of the most flagrant kind. Consequently, it was more than they could countenance and as a result feelings ran high between the two countries.

Yet despite the long-strained relations such conditions had spawned the woman never hesitated to show her faith in Jesus publicly by appealing openly to him to heal her child of an "unclean spirit" — perhaps epilepsy.

## II

Neither of our two New Testament evangelists tells us

33

anything about the woman beyond her plight and her plea. However, her approach to the Master is in itself revealing.

Despite the fact the woman was a foreigner she already knew a great deal about Jesus. Nor is it surprising that she did. For her native land was the geographical center of the New Testament world. Consequently caravans were constantly crossing its borders with news of what was happening in Palestine. Thus, like many among her neighbors, she must have followed with profound interest reports they brought of the Master's activities. As a result, while many of her friends had come to hold what one writer terms a "half-interest" in Jesus as the Messiah, to the concerned mother he was the embodiment of God's love in the world. Now that he was standing in the shadow of Tyre's smoking chimneys she would attest that conviction by publicly seeking his help for her daughter.

The depth of the woman's confidence is evident in the manner in which she addressed Jesus on catching up with him. For unlike the Master's first two disciples whom John the Baptist had directed to him she did not call him "rabbi." (John 1:38) Instead, she called him "Lord" and "Son of David" (Matthew 15:22) — titles distinctive of the true Messiah. It was a striking witness, spontaneously made; and those standing by could not have missed its significance reflecting as it did more faith than his own people were displaying.


### III


Having thus openly acknowledged Jesus as the long-awaited Messiah the woman proceeded to plead her daughter's case. To her dismay Jesus turned a deaf ear to her. (Matthew 15:23) He who had volunteered to heal a woman so badly crippled that she could not walk upright (Luke 10:10-13) was now standing unmoved before a mother holding up to him the affliction of her child.

Compounding matters still further the disciples came up

as the woman was making her appeal and, sizing up the situation, they urged Jesus to send the woman away lest she become troublesome to them all.

Some, recalling the mandate Jesus had delivered to the Twelve as he dispatched them on a missionary journey, (Matthew 10:5-6) think he reacted to the woman's appeal in the manner he did because she was not an Israelite. But the Master loved children and wanted only the best for them. (cf. Matthew 18:16; 19:13-15) So there must have been some other reason for his seeming insensitivity.

And there was.

Jesus was trying to keep a low profile in Canaan. Let word of what he was doing get back to Jerusalem and it could spell disaster for him. For not only had he incurred the wrath of Herod Antipas, thus facing the threat of suffering the same fate as the Tetrarch had meted out to John the Baptist; he had likewise experienced a bitter encounter with a delegation Israel's hierarchy had sent to grill him on his teachings and practices. (Matthew 15:1-8) It had been a trying ordeal, and he desperately felt the need to get away for a while. So he had withdrawn to the relative safety of Tyre and Sidon seeking a respite. (Matthew 15:21) Quite understandably he did not want to do anything that might attract attention to his whereabouts lest his enemies track him down and put a violent end to his mission.

As a result of all this Jesus was emotionally drained, as his disciples apparently realized. For knowing how each of his mighty works depleted his strength, (cf. Mark 5:30) and familiar with the stress under which he was laboring, they urged him to send the woman away. (Matthew 15:23)

The woman refused to go, however, her very persistence a public testimony to the strong faith she had in the Master. Accordingly, instead of quietly withdrawing as the disciples were urging her to do she followed the little band wherever they went, the earnestness of her petition a continuing witness to her faith in the compassion and power of Jesus.

## IV

How long the woman pressed her appeal we have no way of knowing. But one thing is certain. Not only did she believe in the Master's ability to heal her daughter, she was determined to persist until he did. Moreover, she did so without once asking Jesus to divert his steps to the house where her child lay. So far as she was concerned all that mattered was for him to give his word.

Yet still Jesus demurred, his mission to the Jews very much on his mind. "It's not fair to take the children's bread and throw it to the dogs," he said, finally turning to the woman in recognition of her appeal. (Matthew 15:26) It was an answer the woman understood since she was undoubtedly familiar with some of the rabbinical sayings that applied the term "dog" to Gentiles. Nor did she take offense at it, recognizing that he was employing the word figuratively; for the form in which he was using it conjured up the picture of pets circling a table at mealtime in quest of morsels.

It was not that Jesus lacked compassion for Gentiles. It was rather that as the Prince of the House of David he envisioned his mission to Israel as his primary responsibility, (cf. Isaiah 56:7; Mark 11:17) and he must fulfill that responsibility at all costs. Thus, trying as the moment was for the woman, it was not an easy one for the Master either, caught as he was between the woman's persistent petitioning and his heavenly mandate. Or to put it another way, on the one hand he faced the need of an individual, on the other the salvation of a people. And always in the background there were those waiting to trap him.

But the woman refused to be silenced. For as Frederick Farrar expressed it in a day now long since gone, "not all the snows of her native Lebanon could quench the fire of love burning on the altar of her heart." Her child lay desperately ill, and the distraught mother simply refused to believe that he who gathered little children about his feet to bless them would deny her request. (Matthew 19:13-14)

Accordingly, the woman pressed her plea, adroitly employing Jesus' own figure of speech to do so. "Yes, Lord," she replied, "yet even the dogs eat the crumbs that fall from their Master's table." (Matthew 15:27) How deftly she had matched his metaphor! For she was putting human need above race and nationality.

## V

Instantly the woman's reply struck a chord with Jesus, for in effect she was anticipating Peter's declaration to Cornelius that God shows no partiality. (Acts 10:34) And that being so "no case is too desperate for prayer."

It was a conviction Jesus confirmed forthwith. "O woman," he said in a voice all within earshot could clearly hear, "great is your faith: be it unto you as you will." (Matthew 15:28) And the girl was whole again.

Unwavering faith had prevailed. Moreover, it had done so in a very important way. For one thing it had broken down the barrier of a specified point of origin. From now on what mattered was not where one came from but what one needed to experience the fullness of life. For another thing it had broken down distinctions of race and class, giving new emphasis to Ezekiel's affirmation that all souls are God's. (Ezekiel 18:4) Above all, it had lifted up the assurance that whosoever will may come to the throne of grace. (Revelation 21:17)

Who can doubt that in days to come this mother from Canaan never tired of telling anyone who would listen about her ill daughter and the man from Galilee who gave her child a new lease on life? (Mark 7:30)

*A Big Fisherman*

# Peter

He came from the sea, a brawny, boisterous man, who loved nothing better than the spray in his face as he pitted his little craft against a gale, his calloused hands locked on the tiller, a defiant cry on his lips. And when the wild trick was over how he must have boasted of his feat to friends sharing his hearth!

He was an impulsive man, quick to make decisions and equally quick to make mistakes. Yet he never let either stop him. Instead, he plunged straight on, rushing from one concern to another, always in the thick of things, acting first and thinking about them afterward. So, too, he was a man of moods, one moment courageously casting caution to the winds; the next cringing before circumstance.

His name was Simon. Jesus took one look at him and called him "Rock." (Matthew 16:18) The nickname stuck, and Simon entered history as "Petros" — or, more familiarly, Peter.


## I

A popular assumption notwithstanding, Peter was neither uncultured nor uncouth. On the contrary, he possessed a learning and a bearing leading.

Neither was Peter an average fisherman eking out a living with his daily hauls. Rather, with his brother Andrew he was a partner with Salome's James and John in a flourishing fishing business boasting a small fleet. (Mark 1:16; Luke 5:10) Thus, when he reminded Jesus that "we have left everything and followed you" he was speaking of turning his back on no mean enterprise. (Mark 10:28)

To be sure, Peter had his moments of weakness. On occasion even the most valiant among us has a way of disgracing his best; and, like Frederick the Great fleeing in terror from his first battle, Peter was no exception. The chagrin must have haunted him all his days when he remembered how he permitted two servant girls in Caiaphas' courtyard to frighten him into denying he had ever known Jesus. (Matthew 26:69-72, 75) But, like Frederick, too, he went on to surmount his remorse.

## II

Peter was already a religious person before he met Jesus. His association with John the Baptist attests that. He had responded to the Baptist's call to repentance and baptism, and the response had prepared him for discipleship with Jesus. To be sure the preparation had been gradual, but it had also brought him face to face with spiritual reality. Consequently he had become increasingly aware of his capacity to be a mediator for Christ. Not only that. It had likewise awakened him to the realization he had a wide open field in which to exercise the capacity. For he moved freely among Gentiles to whom he was at liberty to present the Master's claims. Nor did he stop with the presentation. Instead, he took a step farther and led them into the fellowship of the church. (Acts 11:1-18)

It was a major step forward for the faith. Hitherto converts to the Master were primarily Jewish, and understandably so. Had not the prophets foretold a Redeemer from the line of David? But Peter had had a vision in which he was instructed to count none unclean. (Acts 10:28)

To be sure, Israel's hierarchy called Peter to task for what he had done. But so successfully did he defend his action that those calling him to account for it ended up glorifying God because of it. (Acts 11:1-18) It was a genuine triumph of one man's faith, attesting as it did that old things were passing away and all things were becoming new. (2 Corinthians 5:17)

## III

Many leaders are forgotten once they are gone, their work perishing with them. Peter was determined that Jesus and his mission would never suffer that fate. One of the first things he did in attesting his faith following the crucifixion, therefore, was to seal the breach Judas' defection had created in the ranks of the Twelve. He had the disciples cast lots to determine a successor to the man from Kerioth. The lot fell on Matthias. (Acts 1:15-26) It was both a spiritual act and a practical stroke, for it put the world on notice that Jesus' ministry to humanity was still very much alive through his followers.

Pentecost came almost on the heels of the big fisherman's action. Nor did he let it pass without bearing his witness to the Parthians and Medes and Elamites and numerous others gathered in Jerusalem from all parts of the Mediterranean. For rising to the occasion he bore his testimony so eloquently that three thousand of their number endorsed "the apostles' teaching and fellowship." (Acts 2:1-42)

Stirring as this event was, however, Peter knew he could not let matters rest there. So he pressed on with his witness by taking steps to conserve the decisions of those who were joining the fellowship daily. (Acts 2:47) From personal experience the big fisherman was aware the converts could not be left to their own devices to grow in the faith. Moreover, had not the Master once told him that by strengthening his brethren he would keep his own faith alive? (Luke 22:31-33)

Unnurtured decisions, Peter realized, dim and die. Accordingly he organized the church and set up a program of training that was to enable the Lord's followers to win the world in 300 years.

That Peter took no small part in this achievement personally is attested by the fact he established what one scholar calls "a long history of travel" as he marched in the church's vanguard seeking the heathen wherever he could find them. One day he was in Samaria, the next Lydda, then on to Joppa and Caesarea. (Acts 8:14-17; 9:32-10:48) And where he could not go personally, time not permitting, he wrote his testimonies — today an epistle from Babylon where Jews were numerous, tomorrow another to Asia Minor. But whether writing his appeal or making it in person Peter was careful to proclaim the law of love with equal vigor.

Nor did Peter neglect Jerusalem while doing all this. Instead, as Henry K. Rowe reminds us, he led his fellow disciples "in a drive on the callous soul of Jerusalem and won many." Here was a man who might give out, but he would never give up. For he had the courage to follow the dictates of his heart, not the least of which was the conviction he held that God was calling him to break down the distinction between Jew and Gentile.

It was a conviction upon which Peter stood ready to act at all times. Consequently, when the Roman soldier Cornelius responded to Peter's preaching and requested baptism at the big fisherman's hands he did not hesitate to administer the sacred rite to both Cornelius and his household.

It was a major step, and the Jerusalem church speedily summoned Peter to defend his action. So effective was his response that those calling him to account ended up glorifying God for what had taken place. (Acts 10:30-48) It was a high moment holding forth great promise for the days to come.

## IV

Peter's witness to Jesus, however, soon cost him something. For it was meeting with such widespread response that it alarmed the authorities who saw in it a threat to their supremacy. After all, Peter was from Galilee, Israel's hotbed of rebellion; and allowed to go unchecked his testimony might very well topple them from power. So they arrested him along with his companions.

Actually, it was the authorities' intent to execute both the big fisherman and his cohorts, and to do so with dispatch. But one of their number, the highly respected lawyer, Gamaliel, intervened, warning his colleagues that they would do well to find out before they did whose side God was on. Otherwise, he cautioned, they may run afoul of the Almighty himself and thus suffer severe consequences at his hands.

Such counsel was enough to stir up second thoughts, and those in power speedily drew back from their original intent, deciding instead to settle for administering a beating to Peter and his companions. Then they turned the group loose with a mandate never to mention Jesus' name again. (Acts 5:17-40)

The mandate was, of course, futile, and even as the authorities issued it they must have sensed it was. Indeed, so effectively did Peter continue to witness "in the temple and at home" that the Lord's followers kept increasing in numbers. (Acts 5:42-6:1)

V

It required no small courage on Peter's part to pick up his evangelizing where the authorities had so threateningly disrupted it. A lesser man would have abandoned the field post-haste. But at heart Peter was a bold man. His attempt to walk on the sea, and his drawing of a sword in the face of hostile soldiers threatening the Master, attest that. (Matthew 14:28-30; John 18:3-10) So he continued to do what he had been doing by way of lifting up the Lord.

At the same time Peter was a sensitive man, especially where Jesus was concerned; and he did not hesitate to show it. (Matthew 16:22) Moreover, he was loyal to Jesus to the end. A fourth-century frieze portrays Peter, under guarded arrest, striking water from a rock in the name of the Master for the baptism of his jailer.

Nor was it Peter's last act of exaltation. Tradition tells us he turned even his death into a witness for Christ by insisting on being crucified head down.

## A Woman Of Substance
# Mary Magdalene

When we first meet Mary Magdalene she is already witnessing to Jesus. Not only so. She is a substantial witness. For she is a member of a band of women supporting the Master out of their own means as they accompany him throughout Galilee (Luke 8:1-3) — in itself no small testimony.

## I

Unfortunately, for 16 centuries Mary has stood unjustly in the shadow of slander. A fourth-century scholar thought he saw a link between Luke's account of a sinful woman seeking Jesus' forgiveness (Luke 7:36-50) and the Evangelist's introduction of Mary's role in the Master's ministry with only two verses of scripture intervening. (Luke 8:1-2) Others around him quickly accepted his conclusion; and, as a result, it took root — so deeply, in fact, that the church of the middle ages went so far as to stage mystery plays portraying Mary "in league with Lucifer" until the Savior miraculously snatched her from the Evil One's clutches. As a consequence Mary's name became a synonym for the word prostitute.

Nothing Jesus ever did or said where Mary was concerned justified the charge. Equally to the point, during the church's first 300 years the Magdalene was highly regarded in its circles. Indeed, wherever scripture or other early Christian writings speak of her she is saluted as one whose presence would grace any gathering of right-minded people. A true "mother of the church" is the way one scholar describes her. Yet another refers to her as holding "a good social position."

Moreover, the gospels call our attention to Mary no fewer than 14 times to bestow upon her a distinction they do not even accord the disciples; for better than half of the Apostles are dismissed with only the notation that "they had been with Jesus."


## II


Where or how Mary attained the means to support the Master in his mission to humanity we are never told. Unlike Salome and Joanna, there is no hint she had a sympathetic husband to underwrite her efforts in the Lord's behalf. It would seem quite logical, therefore, to surmise that, like Lydia of Thyatira, (Acts 16:14) she may have operated a business of her own providing her with a tidy income.

After all, Mary came from Magdala which, like Paul's Tarsus, was "no mean city." (cf. Acts 21:39) For not only was it the center of a flourishing fishing industry, it likewise boasted both a woolen factory and a celebrated dyeworks. In addition, it experienced a brisk traffic in turtledoves for ceremonial purification.

That this latter was no small enterprise seems apparent in the fact tradition, with what is probably Oriental exaggeration, indicates the town had 300 shops engaged in this endeavor. Be that as it may, however, something of the traffic's impact on the area as a whole is suggested by the fact that just twenty minutes north of Magdala caravans plying between Nazareth and Damascus passed through a wady known as the Valley of Doves. In fact, such was Magdala's commerce, as Alfred Edersheim points out, that the city was one of three which forwarded their taxes to Jerusalem by wagon.

These were not the only resources, however, offering Mary Magdalene a favorable climate for any enterprise she may have undertaken. Magdala was located on the western shore of the Sea of Galilee. Accordingly, it was but a Sabbath day's journey — roughly three miles — from Tiberius, whose amphitheaters and public baths made it a veritable "picture of magnificence" as well as a lucrative source of income. Thus, Magdala's proximity to it offered Mary ready access to a variety of thriving commercial opportunities. So the monies she contributed to the support of Jesus' ministry may very well have stemmed from her own labors.

Lending credence to this conjecture is the fact that Mary appears to have been a middle-aged woman when she joined the Master's coterie. To be sure, artists have never tired of portraying her as a lithe, auburn-haired young woman. But nothing in the gospels supports such a concept while first-century practices offer strong evidence against it.

To begin with, Israel's stern code governing women would have required a girl of tender years to be strictly supervised by either her father or a male guardian, holding each severely to account for her conduct. Thus, it is highly improbable Mary would have traveled the countryside with any man — not even a rabbi — had she not been older.

In the second place, Hebrew custom put a premium on seniority. Consequently, it is doubtful the gospel writers would have listed Mary first among the ministering women if she had been the youthful individual painters have so frequently depicted her. Yet, when referring to the women in Jesus' life, the Evangelists often put Mary's name ahead of her colleagues — a practice clearly reflecting the respect her years commanded. (cf. Matthew 27:56, 61; Mark 15:40, 16:1; Luke 24:10) At the same time the practice also suggests that Mary was quite possibly a person of rank and consequently prominent.

Mary's high prestige in Magdala notwithstanding, however, her commitment to Jesus was total. Thus, she would not allow the untoward events Pilate was setting in motion to divert her from it. So she readily joined a little band of weeping women following the Master as he carried his cross like a common criminal to Calvary. Not even the choking dust the sad procession stirred up as it wended its way to the skull-shaped hill could deter her from following. For she was bent on one thing — and one thing only. She would tell Pilate — and in telling

47

him she would tell the world — that Jesus was her Lord. (cf. Luke 23:27; John 20:25)

## III

Be all this as it may, however, Mary Magdalene comes fully into her own on the day of resurrection when supposition yields to biblical history.

Jesus was crucified at noon. By three o'clock he was dead. Except for John, the disciples had fled, locking themselves behind closed doors "for fear of the Jews." (John 19:26-27; 20:10) But Mary, along with Salome and several other women, had stood vigil throughout the entire ordeal, her very manner an open witness to friend and foe alike of her loyalty to the Master. (Matthew 27:55-56) Nor would she leave until she knew what was to become of Jesus' body. When Pilate finally released it to Nicodemus and Joseph of Arimathea she followed to see where the two men would lay him.

Early in the morning of the first day of the week Mary's sad heart brought her back to the tomb. Because of the intervening Sabbath, which had begun just as the entrance stone was rolled into place at the sepulchre, the customary administrations for the dead had been hasty and the Magdalene was intent upon completing the full rites.

To Mary's consternation she found the grave open, Pilate's official seal tattered and fluttering in the breeze. Fearing the worst, she looked about and saw a man a short distance from her. Supposing him to be a gardener, she approached him for a clue to the mystery she was facing. When he called Mary by name she recognized Jesus, and on the wings of joy she sped to share the good news with the disciples. (John 20:15-18)

Not only was Mary Magdalene the first to know of the resurrection, she was likewise the first to bear witness to it to the world. Indeed, so telling was her testimony that the French scholar, Ernest Renan, does not hesitate to declare, "Next after

Jesus, hers was the most essential part in the founding of Christianity.''

According to an early legend Mary later went to Ephesus with John and died there.

*A Patriot*

# Dysmas

To the Evangelists who wrote the first three gospels he is a nameless person, this young patriot sharing the agony of Jesus' last earthly hours. (Matthew 27:39; Mark 15:27; Luke 23:32) Tradition treats him more kindly. It dignifies him with a name. "Dysmas," it whispers.

Nor does tradition stop there. Instead, it presses on to portray Dysmas as a man of great compassion, deeply concerned for the distressed and the downtrodden, who "despised the rich, but did not give to the poor, even burying them" — no common mercy for the times.

## I

A robber in the eyes of Rome, Dysmas was actually a revolutionary — a freedom fighter, if you will — striking blows for liberty wherever and whenever he could against an invader's occupying legions. Here was no midnight prowler sneaking into the homes of sleeping victims, no masked bandit preying on unwary travelers. Here was an Israelite patriot bent on breaking the shackles a foreign tyrant had imposed on his people and paying for the effort with his life.

A steady deterioration in Israel's internal affairs resulting from bitter rivalries for the throne had led to virtual anarchy in the land. As a consequence one after another of the nation's leaders had been forced to flee into hiding, leaving the populace to the ravages of rampant violence. In fact, not a day passed without conditions worsening. Indeed, so bad had things become that, as John A. Scott puts it, the country's "lawlessness and bloodshed can hardly be described or believed," leading the Pharisees to appeal desperately to Caesar for help.

No less a general than the renowned Pompey responded to the appeal and, aided by traitors within Jerusalem's gates, he took control of the city without drawing a sword.

It was a day to live in infamy. For not only did it reduce Israel's borders to the dimensions of a province, it likewise set up a succession of puppet rulers who delighted in harassing the people. Consequently, it was only a short time until guerrilla bands, fired with a passion to avenge the honor of their native land, had sprung up everywhere. Striking swiftly by night, they sabotaged Roman military supplies, burned food depots, and sniped at bivouacked legionnaires. Neither did they hesitate to put to the sword any collaborators they ferreted out in their scouting. Thus Pompey's sweeping victory notwithstanding, Palestine stood in a state of perpetual rebellion.

Since Dysmas' name is never linked directly with any of the leaders in this carnage and pillaging — such as Judas the Galilean, whose "passionate enthusiasm was disastrously contagious" — it would appear his role in the insurgents' relentless assaults aimed at pushing the Romans into the sea was that of a secret agent. (cf. Luke 23:39-41)

## II

A 12th-century tradition tells us Dysmas was a Galilean innkeeper. To the modern mind the term conjures visions of comfortable establishments not unlike the motels dotting our contemporary superhighways. The inns of biblical times, however, were little more than walled campsites adjacent to caravan routes. Set up as hollow squares, they had a single gate, barred at night against the wild animals. Occasionally there was a cloister just inside the square and, where this existed, there were usually two or three rooms to afford protection from cold and inclement weather. Very likely it was one of these cloisters in which there was no room for Joseph and Mary when Jesus was born. (cf. Luke 2:7)

Obviously, such lodgings would have provided little privacy. Thus, any patriotic innkeeper had only to eavesdrop on indiscreet travelers and boasting legionnaires enroute to assignments to pick up valuable information for the guerrillas. So, too, a few subtle questions fed into the flow of campfire gossip must have elicited military secrets on any number of occasions to the advantage of the revolutionaries.

The prospect of Dysmas thus employing innkeeping as a cover becomes all the more intriguing when we recall how Jesus traveled across Palestine preaching his gospel of the Kingdom. (Mark 1:39) For there may very well have been times when, coming to day's end, the Master spent nights in Dysmas' hostelry. Nor would he have shared Dysmas' hospitality without the two of them talking into the wee hours of the morning. (cf. John 3:2) Hence it is quite probable the Preacher and the patriot were not seeing one another for the first time at Calvary. In fact, Dysmas' last words would seem to indicate otherwise.

### III

There is a familiarity to Dysmas' petition that suggests childhood days of running in and out of Joseph's carpenter shop after the typical fashion of boys sharing an adolescent fellowship. Others might salute the Galilean as "Teacher," "Lord," "Son of David," even "Sir." (John 4:11) But Dysmas calls him Jesus, the intimate name by which the Master responded to Joseph and Mary when he was growing up in Nazareth. (Luke 23:42) The very fact that Dysmas invoked him so familiarly at the crucifixion seems to strengthen the likelihood the two had known one another from their youth.

Apparently the passage of the years had done nothing to dim the relationship between Jesus and Dysmas since each seems to have knowledge of what the other was doing, suggesting they had kept in touch through all of their country's travails. For when the third man on Calvary railed at the crucified Jesus, taunting him to work another miracle, Dysmas roundly rebuked him, "Do you not fear God, since you are under the same sentence of condemnation? And we indeed are punished justly; for we are receiving the due reward of our deeds; but this man has done nothing wrong." (Luke 23:40-41) Only one who had followed the Master's career with unbroken interest could have silenced the scoffer with such a sharp reprimand.

In support of this conjecture the Scottish scholar, Alexander Whyte, goes so far as to propose that on various occasions, ascertaining where Jesus was ministering, Dysmas may have disguised himself as a fisherman or a shepherd "to come down to hear the Lord preach." And what he heard he inscribed on his heart — inscribed it so deeply, in fact, that not even the mob howling at the Crucified could drown out Dysmas' witness to the centuries.

Explain Dysmas' last words as we may, however, they are certainly not the cry of a man fearfully facing death. Instead, they are a clear profession of faith in One who has long since opened up new vistas to him by leading him to see that salvation is of the heart and "not of this world." (John 18:36) Here was a faith in which a person could die content, for its promise extended beyond the grave. Moreover, was not Dysmas ending his life in the company of the Lord who had introduced him to the promise?

## IV

The world has always respected the testimony of dying men. Accordingly, when Dysmas affirmed his faith in Jesus from the arms of a cross the calloused centurion charged with carrying out the crucifixion, instinctively fixing his eyes on the Master, cried above the clamor of the crowd, "Truly, this was the son of God." (Matthew 27:54 KJV)

It was a cry of commitment evoked by Dysmas' dying declaration and profoundly significant to Jesus' cause. For as J.

Newton Davies reminds us, the centurion "is the first fruits of that great band of Gentiles who gladly owe allegiance to the Son of Man." (cf. Acts 10)

It is little wonder the church elevated Dysmas to sainthood for his witness, attesting as it did that anybody can enter the Kingdom of God at any time from any place — even from a hill called Calvary. Nor is it surprising that, bestowing on him the name Latro and establishing a church feast in his honor on March 25, it appointed him patron of those condemned to die.

## *A Family Member*

# Salome

She was well named. For Salome was the familiar feminine form of Solomon. But not only did she bear the wise monarch's name. "The mother of Zebedee's children" was every whit as unique as he. The very fact she identified herself with Jesus' little group attested to that. For the two were family, and families often have a way of underestimating their own. Nor were the Master's kin beyond it. For at times Mary had doubts about her son despite the revelations made to her at his birth, (Luke 2:48-51) while his brothers did not hesitate to discredit him openly. (John 7:5) Yet here was Salome committing herself to Jesus as her people's last, best hope.

Watching Jesus grow up Salome had become convinced of his closeness to God. To her it was evident in both his bearing and the depth of his insights belying his years. Consequently, she had committed herself to him in her heart long before she made her resolution known, awaiting only a fitting moment to declare it. Little did she know that when that moment came it would demand a daring step on her part.

### I

It was the Sabbath, and Jesus was preaching in his home synagogue — his only known appearance in Nazareth. (Luke 4:16-30) It was an occasion Salome would not willingly have missed. For one thing, the Master had just returned from forty days of spiritual preparation and, understandably, she was eager to hear what he had to say. His words, however, only infuriated the neighbors among whom he had grown up, kindling in them such a frenzy they rose as a body bent on killing him.

Such a violent display would have sent a lesser woman scurrying to the sanctuary of the family quays. But not Salome. Instead, what she witnessed only sharpened her resolution to support Jesus all the more. It was a daring resolution, for in pursuing it she knew only too well that she was defying two deep-seated prejudices of the day.

For centuries Israel had identified wisdom and authority with age. Gray hair was a badge of knowledge. (Job 32:7) It was a maxim embraced by all the nations of the East. Yet here was Salome committing her life to a self-appointed teacher half her years. (Luke 3:23) To her friends the very thought of doing so was taboo. But Salome refused to let their stance hold her back.

In addition there was a serious question as to the company Salome would be keeping. For in the eyes of her neighbors she was joining a band of tainted women, defiled by the fact that somewhere in their past each had experienced a mental breakdown, the sign of demon-possession, and therefore to be avoided. But all her life Salome had accepted individuals, not for what they had been, but for what they were. So she would permit neither of the two postures on the part of her neighbors to deter her. Instead, she took her place among the women serving the Master and never broke stride with them.

## II

In the course of fulfilling his mission Jesus decided to visit every town and village in Galilee. Accompanying him on this visitation were the Twelve, the women he had healed, and "many others." (Luke 8:1-3) It was an ambitious undertaking; for, in all likelihood, 30 to 40 persons comprised his retinue — no small body considering the fact their journeying would take several months inasmuch as they were traveling afoot, stopping to preach from time to time, and living off the land. That they experienced no major problem along the way seems evident from the fact the scriptures mention none, suggesting careful advance planning in which Salome undoubtedly played no small part. For she would have brought to the mission insights she had attained in the long years she had shared with Zebedee in their family fishery.

To begin with, Salome would have lifted up the need for placing one person in charge of the group's overall concerns. Someone, she would have pointed out, must have the authority to delegate a division of labor among them lest the mission fall into disarray and end in frustration.

Obviously, it was a responsibility that must not be imposed on Jesus. He must be free to meditate and pray. Nor should the disciples be weighted down with it. They must always be available to the Master for other duties.

Salome, on the other hand, had a background for it with years of business experience behind her. Thus, she knew where to find the best markets and how to bargain in them effectively. At the same time she was a reliable judge of the group's needs and could be depended upon to fulfill them. Accordingly it would seem safe to assume that, devoted to Jesus as she was and eager to see the success of his mission, she was chosen as the company's coordinator.

It was a responsibility to which Salome measured up well. For not only did she delegate work essential to the mission's purpose without receiving complaints, she also took on herself her fair share of it. Hence if any grew weary along the way they had but to look at Salome laboring in their midst to find the incentive they needed to persevere.

Twice a day there would be fire beds to lay by scooping out shallow ovals in the fields and ringing them with rocks to support the two-handled cooking pots used for boiling porridge or stewing meat. (1 Samuel 2:13-14) So, too, there would be open flames to kindle for roasting or parching small sheaves of grain. (Ruth 2:14) Occasionally, conditions permitting, there would be mud ovens to construct for the baking of cakes. (Leviticus 2:4)

Often, too, garments must be mended where brambles had snagged them and, when the opportunity arose, laundered by pounding them with stones in a streambed. Thus, from dawn until well after dark the women kept busy; yet, with Salome sharing the burden beside them, not one of them was tempted to abandon the witness of the worker.

## III

Perhaps all too little has been made of the role Salome filled in Jesus' mission. Yet how different its outcome may have been but for her quiet commitment to him. She was there at the beginning when, lacking his family's support, (Mark 3:31-35) Jesus needed encouragement. She was there when many of those following him, finding the demands of discipleship too exacting, "went back, and walked no more with him." (John 6:66) She was there with no concern for her own safety when the knowledge he was a hunted man with a death threat hovering over him weighed heavily upon Jesus. (John 7:25) So it is hardly surprising Salome was there when Jesus returned from the tomb the first Easter morning. (Mark 16:1, 2)

But then Salome had always been there when anything important was happening to Jesus.

It needs to be remembered, however, that Salome did not lack support in doing what she did for the Master. In a day when a man's word was law where his wife's activities were concerned she apparently had the full backing of her husband, Zebedee. For there is no inkling at any point that he tried to bar her from following Jesus.

For one thing Zebedee realized as well as Salome that unless there were someone to minister to the minister during what gave promise of becoming a lengthy and demanding mission the whole enterprise might be jeopardized. At the same time, knowing his wife's talents, he felt the mission was secure in the expertise she was bringing it. Accordingly, in giving her a free hand in it, like John Milton long centuries later, he was content in the knowledge that "they also serve who only stand and wait."

It was a bold stance on Zebedee's part. For in taking it he knew only too well that he risked ostracism for disregarding the strict code Israel imposed upon women by permitting Salome to travel the countryside with a man other than her husband.

# A Quiet Man
## Andrew

Andrew was a quiet man. Perhaps growing up with his boisterous brother, Peter, helped to make him so. But one thing is sure. All Peter's attention-getting bluster notwithstanding, he could not match Andrew's talent for winning friends.

It was a quality Andrew no doubt developed as a junior partner in his father Jonas' fishery where, side by side with men as hard-working as himself, he had frequently shared the frustration of empty nets (Luke 5:5) or the tedium of mending broken ones, (Matthew 4:21) in the process learning a great deal about human nature.

As a result Andrew had developed two qualities that were to mark all his days. The first was accepting persons as he found them. The second was the patience to stand by them until they rose up on their own. No common characteristics these, they undoubtedly led Jesus to tap Andrew as the first of the Twelve.

## I

Those who knew Andrew quickly discovered that his judgments were sound. Impetuous Peter may jump to conclusions. But not Andrew. Practical by nature and given to patience he could listen without prejudice and respond without reproof. Moreover, in doing either, like every good counselor he carefully kept himself in the background. Indeed, so successfully did he do so that even his colleagues forgot to mention him in their memoirs.

At the same time Andrew had no illusions regarding his limitations. Rather, he readily accepted them, confident it was not what a person had but what a person did with what he had that mattered. Thus, he lost no time brooding over his place in the circle of the Twelve. Instead, he would use such gifts as he possessed to the best of his ability convinced God gives us talents, not to compete with our fellows, but to supplement them.

As a consequence it never occurred to Andrew to equate happiness with recognition. James and John may vie for position in the company of the disciples, but Andrew was content just to know that Jesus had enlisted him in the group to work out God's will in the world. Thus, as one writer suggests, his eyes were never in the clouds but rather on the demands and duties of daily life. As a result his approach to people was always positive. It was a stance he had derived in large measure from watching his older brother from whom he had learned that there is more to every individual than meets the eye.

To be sure, Peter had his faults. He was never above speaking out unwisely or rushing rashly into situations he may have more wisely avoided. At the same time, however, he had also possessed a deep-seated empathy requiring only the challenge of another's need to bring out the best in him. Accordingly, long before anxious multitudes lay their afflicted loved ones in the streets for Peter's healing shadow to touch (Acts 5:15-16) Andrew was aware that his brother's crude exterior sheathed a tender heart.

It was an insight to stand Andrew in good stead all his days. For if his own brother possessed such hidden assets, he reasoned, must not others be similarly endowed? So Andrew would pass no judgments drawn from appearances nor harbor prejudices against persons of other nations or races for want of a common culture.

As matters turned out Andrew found himself called upon to exercise these insights in two widely different circumstances.

## II

The first circumstance involved a boy.

Accompanied by the Twelve Jesus had sailed from Capernaum for a "lonely place" on the eastern shore of Galilee seeking a much needed respite. The disciples had just returned from an extensive evangelistic mission on which he had sent them, and they were understandably weary. (Mark 6:7-13) At the same time the crowds were pressing the Master and his small band so persistently that neither he nor the Twelve had had "leisure even to eat." (Mark 6:31-32)

The people, however, had seen the group embark and immediately set out after them. It may be that some in the crowd had overheard the disciples discussing the place for which they were heading. Or the direction the small vessel took on departing Capernaum may have alerted the throng to Jesus' destination. Whatever the case, however, the multitude hastened to catch up with him. Some pursued him in other craft. The larger number traveled afoot around the tip of the lake and actually arrived at Jesus' appointed refuge — the fishing village of Bethsaida — before him (Mark 6:33) since the distance was shorter by land than by water.

Stepping ashore the Master found himself facing more than 5,000 men, women, and children "from all the towns" along the way bent on seeing and hearing him; and, fatigued though he was, he could not bring himself to disappoint them. So he preached to them.

It was late when the sermon ended, (Mark 6:35) and by then the crowd was hungry. The place where the people had gathered, however, was barren and, genuinely concerned, the disciples urged Jesus to send them away to such villages as they may find to obtain food and lodging before darkness overtook them. (Luke 9:12)

Andrew, meanwhile, had struck up an acquaintance with a boy in the crowd; and, learning the lad had five loaves and two fish in a hamper his mother had prepared for him, the Apostle encouraged the boy to take them to Jesus. Perhaps, as J. G. Greenhough suggests, Andrew felt "it was better to give a mouthful of food to a dozen famishing men than to send the whole company empty away." Be that as it may, however, the boy responded as Andrew proposed and so touching was his gesture that hidden lunches rapidly appeared throughout the multitude, setting up a feast for all "with fragments left over." (Matthew 15:29-37; Mark 6:30-44; Luke 9:10-17; John 6:1-14)

## III

The second circumstance calling for Andrew's response occurred when a party of Greeks approached Philip asking to see Jesus. Finding Greek culture laying claims and stirring hopes it was powerless to fulfill they were turning to the Master for spiritual uplift. However, they did not approach him directly. Instead — perhaps because he bore a Greek name — the party went to Philip and requested to be taken to Jesus.

Uncertain of his ground, Philip was reluctant to do as the Greeks asked. But neither would his sense of courtesy permit him to deny them the audience they sought. So, to settle the issue he led them to Andrew, who immediately recognized the significance of the situation. For he saw in it not simply a handful of Greeks seeking an interview with Jesus, but rather the Gentile world flinging its doors wide to the Lord's coming. Viewing the situation in this light, he was quick to make the introduction Philip had so cautiously evaded.

It was a highly significant stand on Andrew's part. For in taking it he was refusing to rule out for foreigners the hope Jesus was offering Israel. At the same time neither would he countenance the thought of the Twelve existing as a closed and ingrown group.

Neither was Andrew's action without its fruits. On the contrary it added a new dimension to the Apostles' thinking by introducing them to a world view which, according to tradition, ultimately gave rise to the Apostles parceling out the nations for evangelizing, an act which in itself constituted no small step toward laying a foundation for the Kingdom the righteous awaited. (cf. Matthew 28:19)

66

Nor did Andrew drop matters there. Rather, following his vision of the Master's mission embracing the nations he took a step farther. He went himself with Jesus' offer of the transformed life to Epirus, Scythia, and Greece, even though he knew he was putting his life at risk in doing so. Thus, as one scholar reminds us, he became the church's first missionary.

But in the process Andrew also became the church's first martyr. For when he went to Greece his preaching so enraged the country's proconsul that he had Andrew crucified on an X-shaped cross.

# A Cloud Of Witnesses

Witnesses die. But the witness lives on.

To borrow a phrase from the nameless writer of the Letter to the Hebrews (11:32) "time would fail us to tell" of Paul carrying the witness throughout the Mediterranean world, of Patrick turning his native Ireland into an "Isle of Saints," of Augustine holding a blueprint of heaven before a pagan Rome, of Martin Luther alerting Germany to a grace realized by faith, of John Wesley offering a "new, best hope" to a jaded England, of Francis Asbury forging a trail across an American wilderness to bring the promise of God's redeeming love to its scattered settlers, of Albert Schweitzer combining medical skill with spiritual concern to drive sinister powers from Africa, of L. P. Larsen and Charles Andrews between them, the one in the south, the other in the north, attesting the Christian way to India — witnesses all to the purpose and compassion of the Galilean.

Perhaps Edward Thring of Uppingham expresses it best when he declares:

> 'neath the Eternal Eyes
> One human joy shall touch the just
> To know their spirit's heirs arise
> And lift their purpose from the dust;
> The father's passion arms the son
> And the great deed goes on, goes on.